The Missing
Diary
of
Admiral Richard E. Byrd

THE MISSING DIARY OF ADMIRAL RICHARD E. BYRD

A Secret Expedition and Journey to a Paradise Inside the Earth

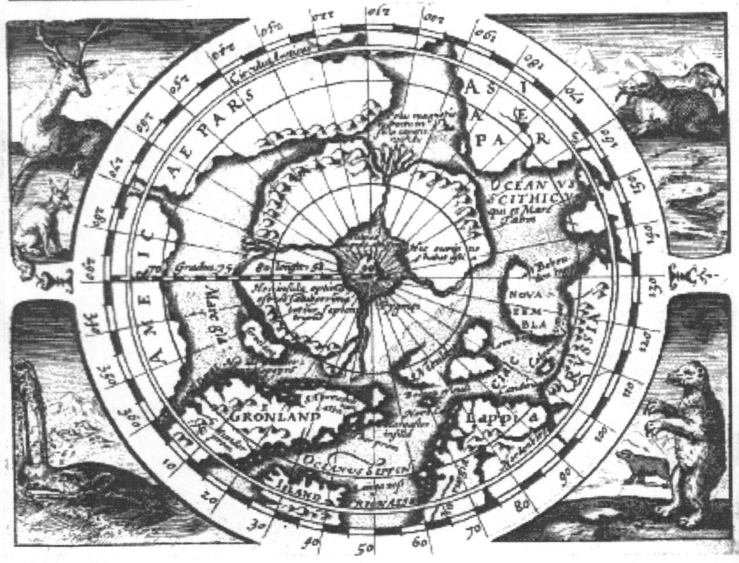

The Missing
Diary
of
Admiral Richard E. Byrd

POST OFFICE BOX 753
NEW BRUNSWICK, NJ 08903

The Missing Diary of Admiral Richard E. Byrd

Timothy Green Beckley: Editorial Director
Carol Rodriguez: Publisher's Assistant
Associate Editors: Sean Casteel and Tim Swartz
Special Thanks: William Kern

Printed in the United States of America

For Free Subscription To The Conspiracy Journal Write:

Global Communications
Box 753
New Brunswick, NJ 08903

Sign Up Online: MRUFO8@hotmail.com

www.ConspiracyJournal.Com

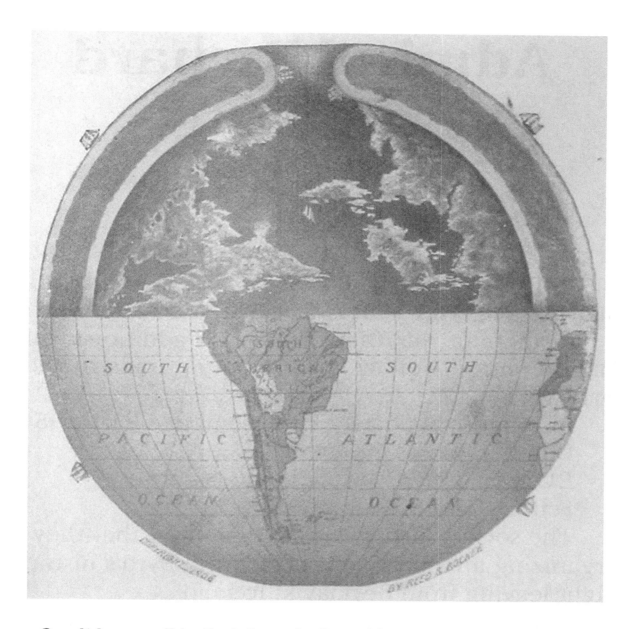

Can it be possible that down in the middle of the Earth there is another Earth? That a few hundred miles or so away, separated from us by ground and rock and vapor and such things, there is a great country inhabited by a great race?

The Missing Diary of Admiral Richard E. Byrd

RECREATION OF ADMIRAL RICHARD BYRD'S HISTORICAL FLIGHT PLANNED BY THE INTERNATIONAL SOCIETY FOR A COMPLETE EARTH

Readers of this Diary who wish additional information on the Hollow Earth theory are instructed to write to:

International Society for a Complete Earth (ISCE)
Danny L. Weiss (Secretary)
P.O. Box 890
Felton, Calif 05018

The society also wishes to announce that they are organizing a reenactment of Admiral Byrd's historical flight leaving from Reykjavik, Iceland.

The flight will be filled with mystery and the potential of discovery. It will follow precisely the route taken by the Admiral and his crew. Each landmark will be pointed out indicating the stress, excitement and frustration that the Admiral was experiencing in the Diary's Log.

The Exploration Flight
Over the North Pole

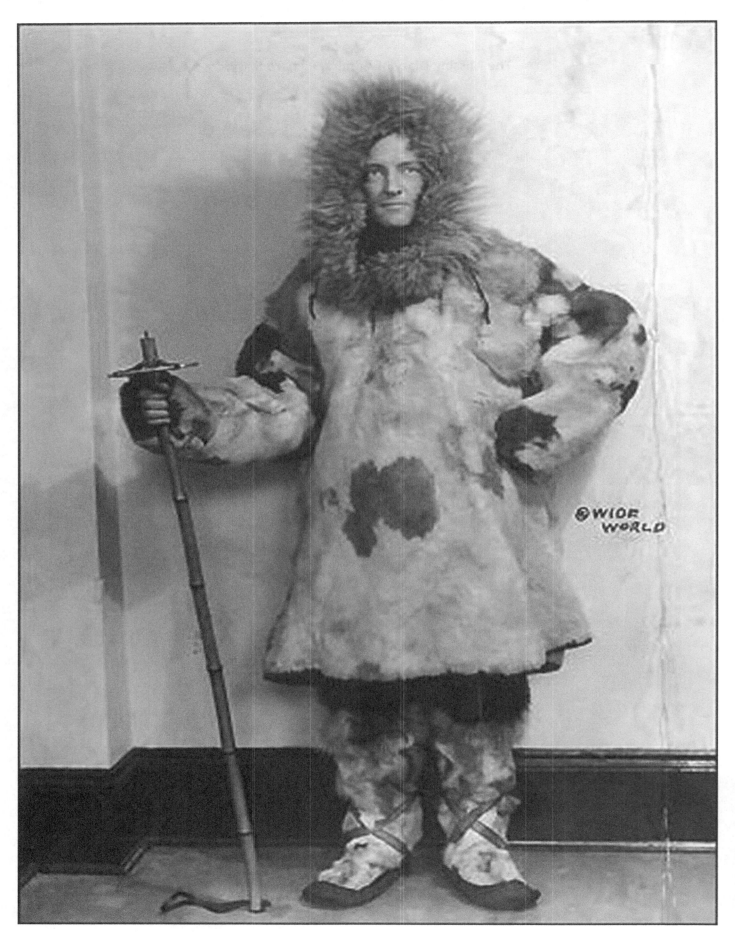

I must write this diary in secrecy and obscurity. It concerns my Arctic flight of the nineteenth day of February in the year of Nineteen and Forty Seven.

The earth as it would appear if viewed from space showing the north polar opening to the planet's interior which is hollow and contains a central sun instead of an ocean of liquid lava.

There comes a time when the rationality of men must fade into insignificance and one must accept the inevitability of the Truth!

I am not at liberty to disclose the following documentation at this writing... perhaps it shall never see the light of public scrutiny, but I must do my duty and record here for all to read one day.

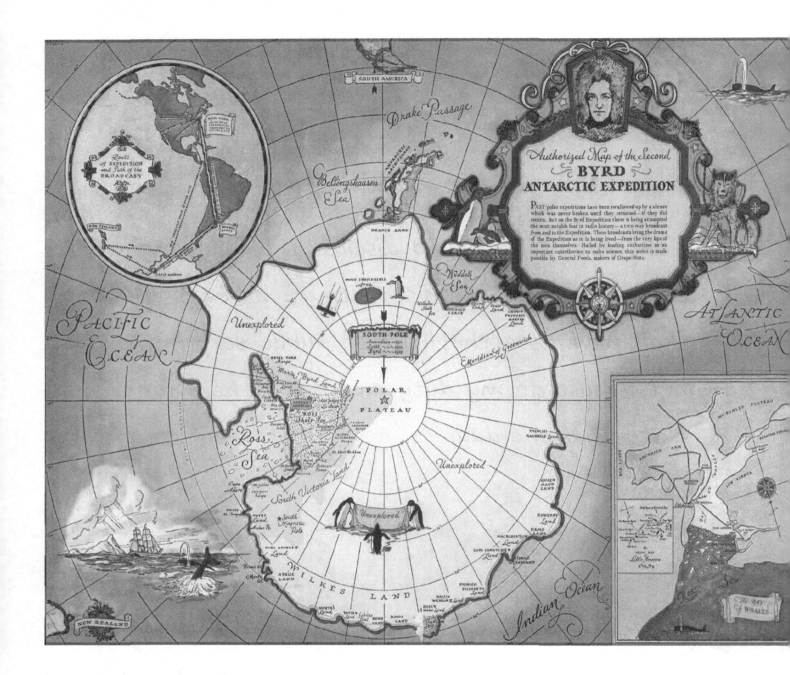

In a world of greed and exploitation of certain of mankind can no longer suppress that which is truth.

Photo # 306-NT-549A-2 Commander Richard E. Byrd, USN

FLIGHT LOG – BASE CAMP ARCTIC

February 19, 1947

0600 Hours— All preparations are complete for our flight north ward and we are airborne with full fuel tanks at 0610 Hours.

0620 Hours– fuel mixture on starboard engine seems too rich, adjustment made and Pratt Whittneys are running smoothly.

0730 Hours- Radio Check with base camp.
All is well and radio reception is normal.

0740 Hours- Note slight oil leak in starboard engine, oil pressure indicator seems normal, however.

0800 Hours- Slight turbulence noted from easterly direction at altitude of 2321 feet, correction to 1700 feet, no further turbulence, but tail wind increases, slight adjustment in throttle controls, aircraft performing very well now.

DRAMA OF HUMAN DARING AND COURAGE
AT THE BOTTOM OF THE WORLD!

WITH BYRD AT THE SOUTH POLE

ACTUALLY FILMED
IN THE VAST UNKNOWN
OF THE ANTARCTIC

a Paramount Picture

0815 Hours– Radio Check with base camp, situation normal.

0830 Hours– Turbulence encountered again, increase altitude to 2900 feet, smooth flight conditions again.

0910 Hours– Vast Ice and snow below, note coloration of yellowish nature, and disperse in a linear pattern. Altering course foe a better examination of this color pattern below, note reddish or purple color also.

Circle this area two full turns and return to assigned compass heading. Position check made again to base camp, and relay information concerning colorations in the Ice and snow below.

0910 Hours- Both Magnetic and Gyro compasses beginning to gyrate and wobble, we are unable to hold our heading by instrumentation. Take bearing with Sun compass, yet all seems well. The controls are seemingly slow to respond and have sluggish quality, but there is no indication of Icing!

0915 Hours- In the distance is what appears to be mountains.

0949 Hours- 29 minutes elapsed flight time from the first sighting of the mountains, it is no illusion. They are mountains and consisting of a small range that I have never seen before!

0955 Hours- Altitude change to 2950 feet, encountering strong turbulence again.

1000 Hours– We are crossing over the small mountain range and still proceeding northward as best as can be ascertained. Beyond the mountain range is what appears to be a valley with a small river or stream running through the center portion. There should be no green valley below! Something is definitely wrong and abnormal here!

We should be over Ice and Snow! To the portside are great forests growing on the mountain slopes. Our navigation Instruments are still spinning, the gyroscope is oscillating back and forth!

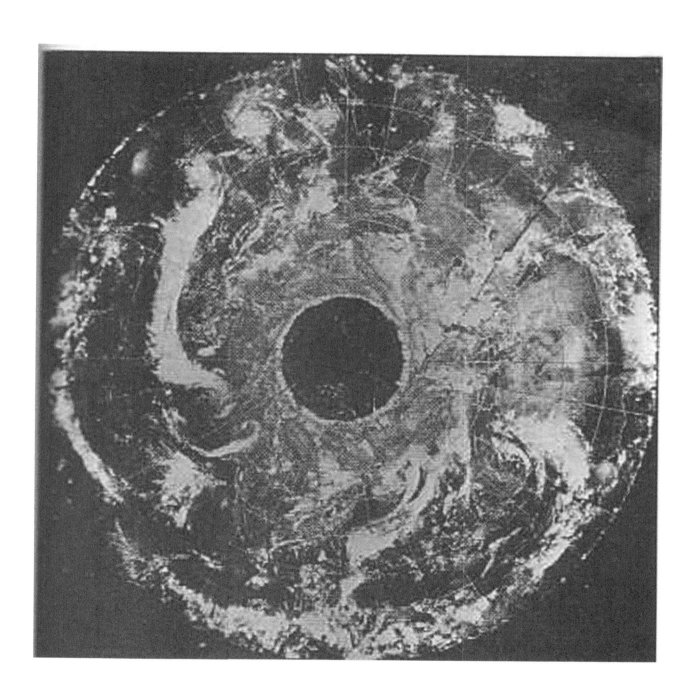

1005 Hours– I alter altitude to 1400 feet and execute a sharp left turn to better examine the valley below. It is green with either moss or a type of tight knit grass. The Light here seems different. I cannot see the Sun anymore. We make another left turn and we spot what seems to be a large animal of some kind below us.

It appears to be an elephant! NO!!! It looks more like a mammoth! This is incredible! Yet, there it is!

Decrease altitude to 1000 feet and take binoculars to better examine the animal. It is confirmed – it is definitely a mammoth-like animal! Report this to base camp.

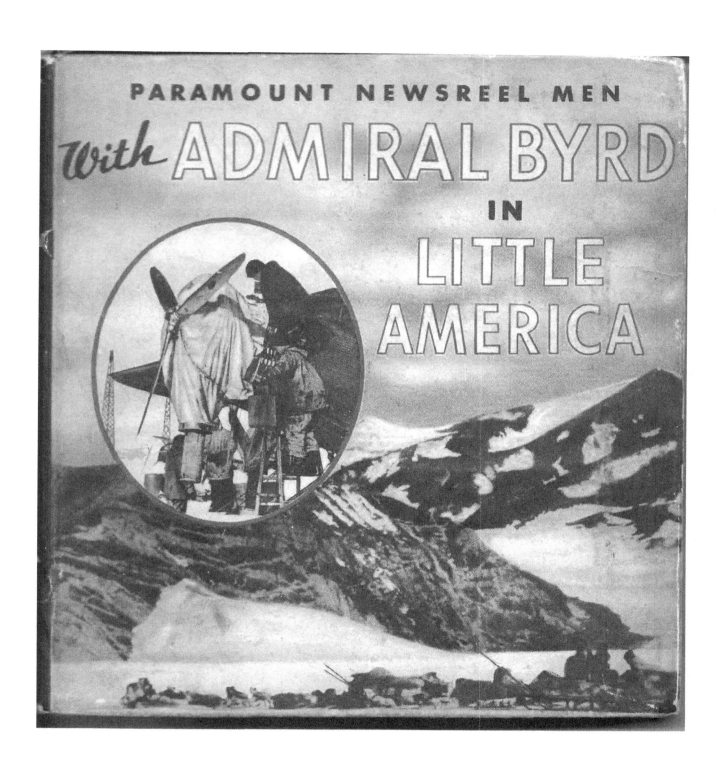

PARAMOUNT NEWSREEL MEN

With ADMIRAL BYRD

IN

LITTLE AMERICA

1030 Hours— Encountering more rolling green hills now. The external temperature indicator reads 74 degrees Fahrenheit! Continuing on our heading now. Navigation instruments seem normal now. I am puzzled over their actions. Attempt to contact base camp. Radio is not functioning!

1130 Hours- Countryside below is more level and normal (if I may use that word). Ahead we spot what seems to be a city!!!! This is impossible! Aircraft seems light and oddly buoyant. The controls refuse to respond!! My GOD!!! Off our port and star board wings are a strange type of aircraft. They are closing rapidly alongside!

They are disc-shaped and have a radiant quality to them. They are close enough now to see the markings on them. It is a type of Swastika!!! This is fantastic. Where are we! What has happened. I tug at the controls again. They will not respond!!!! We are caught in an invisible vice grip of some type!

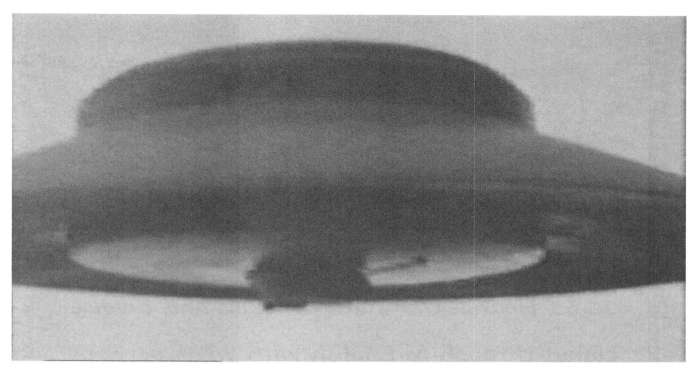

1135 Hours- Our radio crackles and a voice comes through in English with what perhaps is a slight Nordic or Germanic accent! The message is:

'Welcome, Admiral, to our domain. We shall land you in exactly seven minutes! Relax, Admiral, you are in good hands.'

I note the engines of our plane have stopped running! The aircraft is under some strange control and is now turning itself. The controls are useless.

1140 Hours— Another radio message received. We begin the landing process now, and in moments the plane shudders slightly, and begins a descent as though caught in some great unseen elevator! The downward motion is negligible, and we touchdown with only a slight jolt!

1145 Hours- I am making a hasty last entry in the flight log. Several men are approaching on foot toward our aircraft. They are tall with blond hair. In the distance is a large shimmering city pulsating with rainbow hues of color.

I do not know what is going to happen now, but I see no signs of weapons on those approaching. I hear now a voice ordering me by name to open the cargo door. I comply.

END LOG

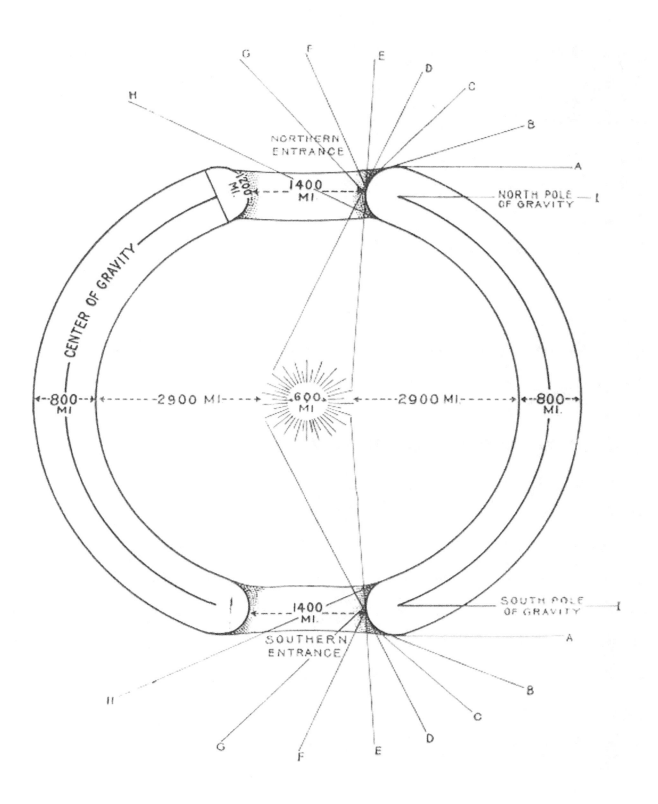

From this point I write all the following events here from memory. It defies the imagination and would seem all but madness if it had not happened.

The radioman and I are taken from the aircraft and we are received in a most cordial manner. We were then boarded on a small platform-like conveyance with no wheels! It moves us toward the glowing city with great swiftness. As we approach, the city seems to be made of a crystal material.

Soon we arrive at a large building that is a type I have never seen before. It appears to be right out of the design board of Frank Lloyd Wright, or perhaps more correctly, out of a Buck Rogers setting!! We are given some type of warm beverage which tasted like nothing I have ever savored before. It is delicious.

After about ten minutes, two of our wondrous appearing hosts come to our quarters and announce that I am to accompany them. I have no choice but to comply. I leave my radioman behind and we walk a short distance and enter into what seems to be an elevator.

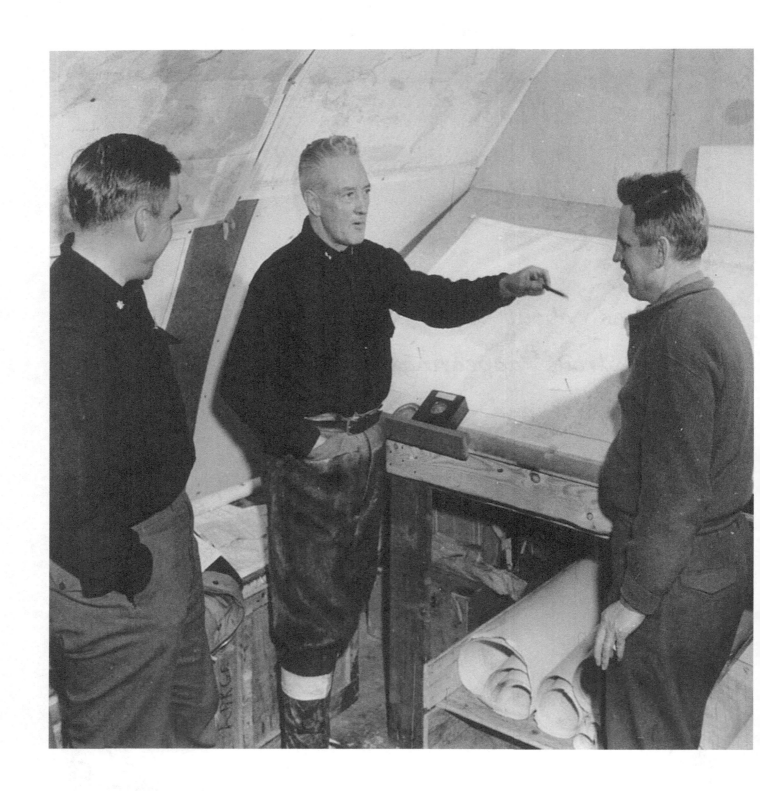

We descend downward for some moments, the machine stops, and the door lifts silently upward! We then proceed down a long hallway that is lit by a rose-colored light that seems to be emanating from the very walls themselves!

One of the beings motions for us to stop before a great door. Over the door is an inscription that I cannot read. The great door slides noiselessly open and I am beckoned to enter.

One of my hosts speaks. 'Have no fear, Admiral, you are to have an audience with the Master...'

I step inside and my eyes adjust to the beautiful coloration that seems to be filling the room completely.

Then I begin to see my surroundings. What greeted my eyes is the most beautiful sight of my entire existence. It is in fact too beautiful and wondrous to describe. It is exquisite and delicate. I do not think there exists a human term that can describe it in any detail with justice!

My thoughts are interrupted in a cordial manner by a warm rich voice of melodious quality, 'I bid you welcome to our domain, Admiral.'

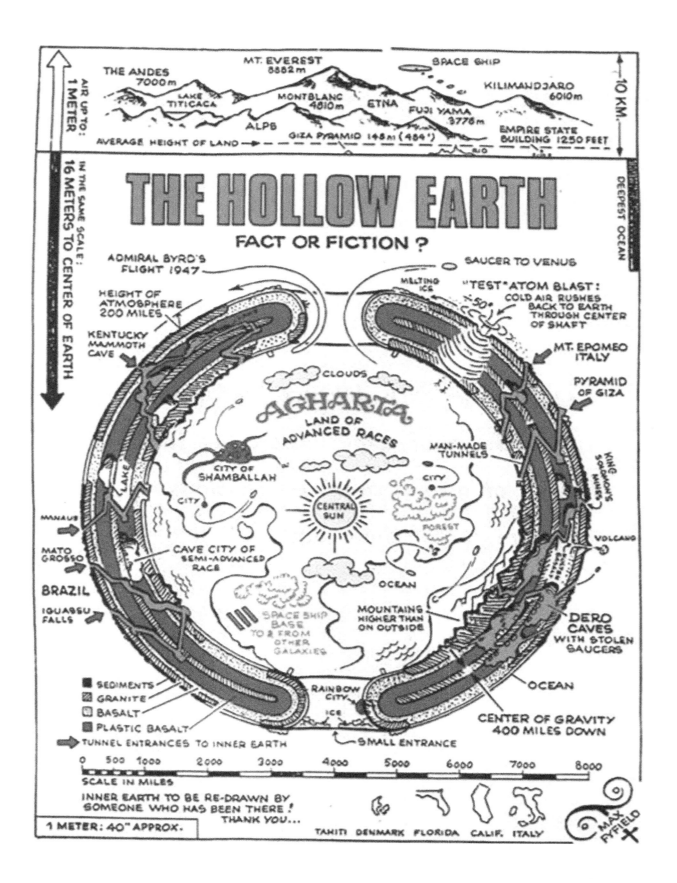

I see a man with delicate features and with the etching of years upon his face. He is seated at a long table. He motions me to sit down in one of the chairs.

After I am seated, he places his fingertips together and smiles. He speaks softly again, and conveys the following:

'We have let you enter here because you are of noble character and well-known on the Surface World, Admiral.'

Surface World, I half-gasp under my breath!

'Yes,' the Master replies with a smile, 'you are in the domain of the Arianni, the Inner World of the Earth. We shall not long delay your mission, and you will be safely escorted back to the surface and for a distance beyond. But now, Admiral, I shall tell you why you have been summoned here.

Our interest rightly begins just after your race exploded the first atomic bombs over Hiroshima and Nagasaki, Japan. It was at that alarming time we sent our flying machines, the "Flugelrads", to your surface world to investigate what your race had done. That is, of course, past history now, my dear Admiral, but I must continue on.

You see, we have never interfered before in your race's wars, and barbarity, but now we must, for you have learned to tamper with a certain power that is not for man, namely, that of atomic energy.

Our emissaries have already delivered messages to the powers of your world, and yet they do not heed. Now you have been chosen to be witness here that our world does exist. You see, our Culture and Science is many thousands of years beyond your race, Admiral.'

I interrupted, 'But what does this have to do with me, Sir?'

The Master's eyes seemed to penetrate deeply into my mind, and after studying me for a few moments he replied, 'Your race has now reached the point of no return, for there are those among you who would destroy your very world rather than relinquish their power as they know it...'

I nodded, and the Master continued, 'In 1945 and afterward, we tried to contact your race, but our efforts were met with hostility, our Flugelrads were fired upon.

Yes, even pursued with malice and animosity by your fighter planes. So, now, I say to you, my son, there is a great storm gathering in your world, a black fury that will not spend itself for many years. There will be no answer in your arms, there will be no safety in your science.

It may rage on until every flower of your culture is trampled, and all human things are leveled in vast chaos. Your recent war was only a prelude of what is yet to come for your race. We here see it more clearly with each hour...do you say I am mistaken?'

'No,' I answer, 'it happened once before, the dark ages came and they lasted for more than five hundred years.'

'Yes, my son,' replied the Master, 'the dark ages that will come now for your race will cover the Earth like a pall, but I believe that some of your race will live through the storm, beyond that, I cannot say.

We see at a great distance a new world stirring from the ruins of your race, seeking its lost and legendary treasures, and they will be here, my son, safe in our keeping. When that time arrives, we shall come forward again to help revive your culture and your race.

Perhaps, by then, you will have learned the futility of war and its strife...and after that time, certain of your culture and science will be returned for your race to begin anew. You, my son, are to return to the Surface World with this message...'

With these closing words, our meeting seemed at an end. I stood for a moment as in a dream....but, yet, I knew this was reality, and for some strange reason I bowed slightly, either out of respect or humility, I do not know which.

Suddenly, I was again aware that the two beautiful hosts who had brought me here were again at my side.

'This way, Admiral,' motioned one.

I turned once more before leaving and looked back toward the Master. A gentle smile was etched on his delicate and ancient face.

'Farewell, my son,' he spoke, then he gestured with a lovely, slender hand a motion of peace and our meeting was truly ended.

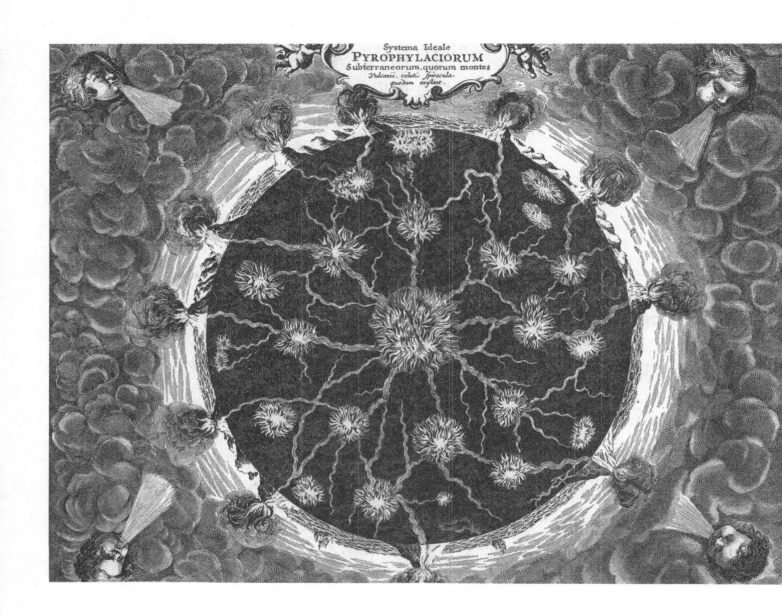

Quickly, we walked back through the great door of the Master's chamber and once again entered into the elevator.

The door slid silently downward and we were at once going upward. One of my hosts spoke again, 'We must now make haste, Admiral, as the Master desires to delay you no longer on your scheduled timetable and you must return with his message to your race.'

I said nothing. All of this was almost beyond belief, and once again my thoughts were interrupted as we stopped. I entered the room and was again with my radioman. He had an anxious expression on his face.

As I approached, I said, 'It is all right, Howie, it is all right.'

The two beings motioned us toward the awaiting conveyance, we boarded, and soon arrived back at the aircraft. The engines were idling and we boarded immediately.

The whole atmosphere seemed charged now with a certain air of urgency. After the cargo door was closed the aircraft was immediately lifted by that unseen force until we reached an altitude of 2700 feet. Two of the aircraft were alongside for some distance guiding us on our return way.

I must state here, the airspeed indicator registered no reading, yet we were moving along at a very rapid rate.

215 Hours – A radio message comes through.

'We are leaving you now, Admiral, your controls are free. Auf Wiedersehen!!!!'

We watched for a moment as the flugelrads disappeared into the pale blue sky.

The aircraft suddenly felt as though caught in a sharp downdraft for a moment. We quickly recovered her control. We do not speak for some time, each man has his thoughts...

ENTRY IN FLIGHT LOG CONTINUES

To my friend
Harald Wilson
who made such
a great contribution
to the success of the
U. S. antarctic service
Richard E Byrd

220 Hours- We are again over vast areas of ice and snow, and approximately 27 minutes from base camp. We radio them, they respond. We report all conditions normal....normal. Base camp expresses relief at our re-established contact.

300 Hours- We land smoothly at base camp. I have a mission...

END LOG ENTRIES

March 11, 1947

I have just attended a staff meeting at the Pentagon. I have stated fully my discovery and the message from the Master.

All is duly recorded. The President has been advised. I am now detained for several hours (six hours, thirty- nine minutes, to be exact.) I am interviewed intently by Top Security Forces and a medical team. It was an ordeal!!!!

I am placed under strict control via the national security provisions of this United States of America. I am ORDERED TO REMAIN SILENT IN REGARD TO ALL THAT I HAVE LEARNED, ON THE BEHALF OF HUMANITY!!! Incredible!

I am reminded that I am a military man and I must obey orders.

December 30, 1956 – FINAL ENTRY

These last few years elapsed since 1947 have not been kind...

I now make my final entry in this singular diary. In closing, I must state that I have faithfully kept this matter secret as directed all these years. It has been completely against my values of moral right. Now, I seem to sense the long night coming on and this secret will not die with me, but as all truth shall, it will triumph and so it shall.

This can be the only hope for mankind. I have seen the truth and it has quickened my spirit and has set me free! I have done my duty toward the monstrous military industrial complex.

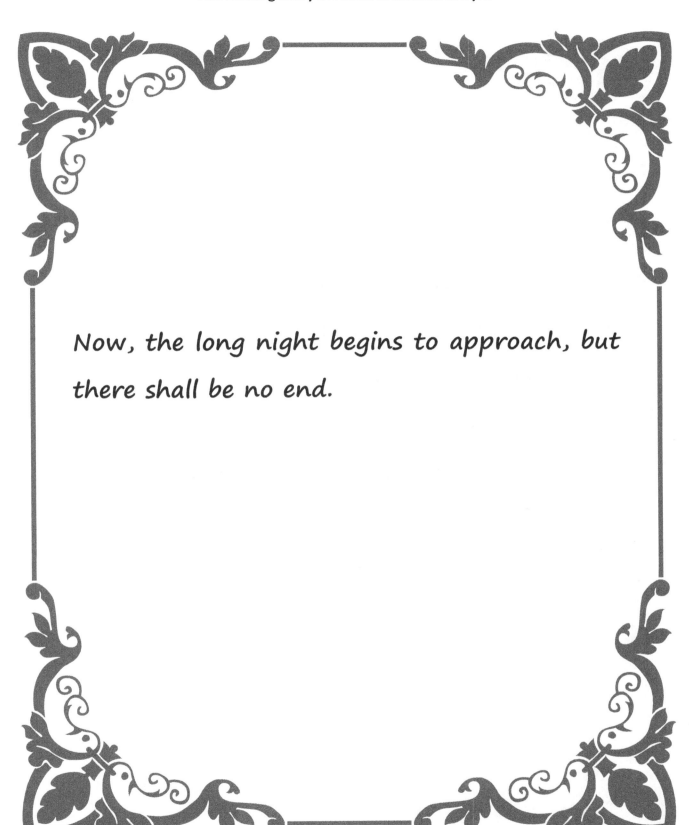

Now, the long night begins to approach, but there shall be no end.

Just as the long night of the Arctic ends, the brilliant sunshine of Truth shall come again... and those who are of darkness shall fall in its Light... FOR I HAVE SEEN THAT LAND BEYOND THE POLE, THAT CENTER OF THE GREAT UNKNOWN.

Admiral Richard E. Byrd

United States Navy

24 December 1956

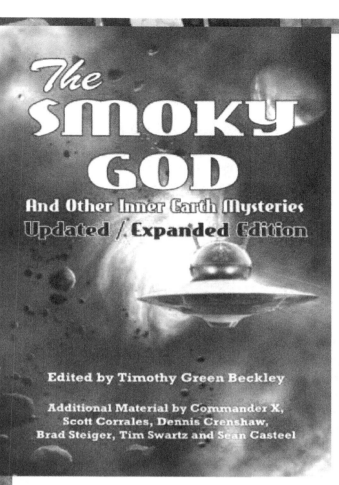

REVELATIONS ABOUT A BLOCKBUSTER DISCOVERY –

SCIENCE BE DAMNED! OUR PLANET IS HOLLOW AND LIFE EXISTS AT THE EARTH'S CENTER AND THROUGH-OUT A VAST TUNNEL SYSTEM.

THE INTERIOR OF THE EARTH IS NOT MADE UP OF MOLTEN LAVA, BUT HOUSES A VAST CIVILIZATION UNHEARD OF BY THOSE LIVING ON THE PLANET'S OUTER SURFACE.

A rare, but all-too-true book, THE SMOKY GOD, tells of a fantastic journey made inside the Earth where the author meets a race of giants who befriend him. This valuable manuscript was believed to be lost for all time but is now available in its entirety, along with other incredible material that provides important evidence that our Earth is hollow and popu-lated by a super race believed to be related to those who once resided on the continents of Lemuria and Atlantis.

Also included in this monumental work:

** The first interview ever with the princess of the underground city beneath Mount Shasta. ** A full description of the Agharta Network, its major cities, language, government, transportation, fi-nancial system, childbirth, age and Ascension. ** Underground locations of alien and Atlantean encampments and the existence of motherships and crystals the size of a New York City sky-scraper.

* A fully-ordained minister's examination of Biblical references to the inner earth and its popu-lation of ten million, as well as the story of an ongoing war between inner earth and outer space people. ** An assessment of what one government official calls a "foreign military incursion" of British and American agents who show an inordinate interest in subterranean tunnels in which paranormal and "unusual" events have been known to transpire on a regular basis. ** How the discovery of one South American tunnel system caused this national government to declare that this discovery "may change our perspective of history!" ** Revelations regarding the existence of ancient mind reading "telog" devices that can scan your home and your brain, as well as other technologically advanced devices that go back thousand and thousands of years but which still ex-ist underground.

VENTURE TO AN UNSEEN WORLD TIME HAS FORGOTTEN! THIS IS THE MOST CENSORED BREAKTHROUGH NEWS OF ALL TIME!

Order THE SMOKY GOD EXPANDED EDITION

(NOW OVER 350 PAGES!) $20.00 + $5.00 S/H From

Timothy Beckley · Box 753 · New Brunswick, NJ 08903

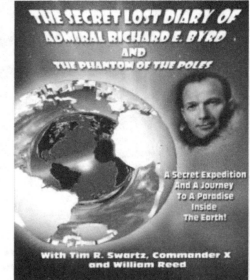

Made in the USA
Las Vegas, NV
14 November 2023

80764204R00070